At the Construction Site

Look, a Flatbed Truck!

T0025457

By Julia Jaske

2

A flatbed truck can carry
many objects.

A flatbed truck can carry
few objects.

4

A flatbed truck can carry
small objects.

A flatbed truck can carry
big objects.

A flatbed truck can carry
small pipes.

A flatbed truck can carry
big pipes.

A flatbed truck can carry
machines.

A flatbed truck can carry cars.

A flatbed truck can carry hay.

A flatbed truck can carry wood.

A flatbed truck can carry logs.

A flatbed truck can carry boxes. 13

Word List

flatbed	big	hay
truck	small	wood
many	pipes	logs
objects	machines	boxes
few	cars	

A flatbed truck can carry many objects.

A flatbed truck can carry few objects.

A flatbed truck can carry small objects.

A flatbed truck can carry big objects.

A flatbed truck can carry small pipes.

A flatbed truck can carry big pipes.

A flatbed truck can carry machines.

A flatbed truck can carry cars.

A flatbed truck can carry hay.

A flatbed truck can carry wood.

A flatbed truck can carry logs.

A flatbed truck can carry boxes.

CHERRY BLOSSOM PRESS

Published in the United States of America by Cherry Lake Publishing Group
Ann Arbor, Michigan
www.cherrylakepublishing.com

Photo Credits: © David Touchtone/Shutterstock, cover, 1, 14; Pusteflower9024/Shutterstock, back cover;
© Everett Media/Shutterstock, 2; © Robert Pernell/Shutterstock, 3; © Bjoern Wylezich/Shutterstock, 4;
© Everett Media/Shutterstock, 5; © rCarner/Shutterstock, 6; © John And Penny/Shutterstock, 7; © Bjoern
Wylezich/Shutterstock, 8; © Bjoern Wylezich/Shutterstock, 9; © TFoxFoto/Shutterstock, 10; © Eric Buermeyer/
Shutterstock, 11; © Noel V. Baebler/Shutterstock, 12; © F Armstrong Photography/Shutterstock, 13

Cherry Blossom Press is an imprint of Cherry Lake Publishing Group.

Library of Congress Cataloging-in-Publication Data

Names: Jaske, Julia, author.
Title: Look, a flatbed truck! / by Julia Jaske.
Description: Ann Arbor, Michigan : Cherry Lake Publishing, [2021] | Series:
  At the construction site
Identifiers: LCCN 2021007851 (print) | LCCN 2021007852 (ebook) | ISBN
  9781534188211 (paperback) | ISBN 9781534189614 (pdf) | ISBN
  9781534191013 (ebook)
Subjects: LCSH: Flatbed trucks—Juvenile literature.
Classification: LCC TL230.15 .J3725 2021 (print) | LCC TL230.15 (ebook) |
  DDC 629.224—dc23
LC record available at https://lccn.loc.gov/2021007851
LC ebook record available at https://lccn.loc.gov/2021007852

Printed in the United States of America
Corporate Graphics